AI Compliance, Reporting & Government Filings

How AI Keeps Your Business Legal & Clean

AF849206

By Joe Correa

Published by Live Stronger Faster

This book is for educational and informational purposes only. The author and publisher are not engaged in rendering legal, financial, tax, or other professional advice. Readers should consult a qualified professional before making any financial decisions.

First Edition

Table of Contents

Introduction

In the modern business world, compliance is no longer just a back-office obligation—it is a strategic pillar of survival, growth, and valuation. Governments now move faster, audit smarter, and monitor businesses more closely than ever before, using data matching, real-time reporting systems, digital tax platforms, and algorithmic risk scoring to detect errors, late filings, inconsistencies, and fraud. In this environment, even honest businesses face enormous exposure simply because of complexity. Every payroll report, every sales-tax return, every information filing, every licensing document, every financial disclosure creates a digital footprint that regulators track across agencies. A single mismatch between your accounting system, tax filings, payroll provider, bank statements, and government databases can trigger fines, penalties, audits, frozen accounts, or worse. Book 8 of the *AI Business & Corporate Tax Optimization* series exists because artificial intelligence is now the only realistic way for businesses to stay compliant at scale, across jurisdictions, and in real time while still growing profitably.

For decades, compliance was built around manual systems: accountants compiling reports, payroll clerks submitting forms, controllers reconciling accounts, and compliance officers checking boxes against regulatory calendars. That model worked when businesses were simpler and when governments moved slowly. Today, businesses operate online, across states and countries, with multiple payment processors, subscription platforms, digital products, contractors, employees, affiliates, and global customers. Every one of those activities triggers reporting obligations—from sales tax nexus filings and VAT returns to payroll reports, contractor 1099s, corporate income taxes, annual reports, franchise taxes, BOI disclosures, and regulatory registrations. Without AI, managing this web of obligations becomes a never-ending game of catch-up, where filings are late, data is wrong, and penalties quietly accumulate. Artificial intelligence changes this by converting compliance from a reactive burden into a proactive, automated system that continuously monitors, prepares, verifies, and submits what governments require.

AI-powered compliance systems do not simply file forms; they create a living, breathing regulatory map of your business. They track where you operate, where you sell, where you hire, where you collect tax, and where you are legally registered. They know your entity type, your tax elections, your payroll obligations, and your reporting cycles. They pull data directly from your accounting, payroll, banking, invoicing, ecommerce, and CRM platforms, ensuring that what you report to governments matches what actually happened in your business. This eliminates one of the most dangerous risks in modern compliance: data mismatch. Most audits and penalties do not begin with fraud—they begin when government databases detect inconsistencies. AI ensures your numbers reconcile before regulators ever see them.

One of the most powerful aspects of AI compliance is its ability to manage regulatory calendars automatically. Businesses today are subject to hundreds of potential deadlines across federal, state, local, and international agencies. Missing even one can lead to penalties, interest, license suspensions, or loss of good standing. AI systems continuously track filing deadlines, renewal dates, reporting obligations, and regulatory changes, alerting you in advance, preparing required documents, and in many cases submitting them automatically. This turns compliance from a stressful guessing game into a predictable, controlled workflow that protects your company's legal standing and financial health.

AI also transforms how businesses handle information returns and third-party reporting. Governments increasingly rely on third-party data—payment processors, payroll companies, banks, and platforms—to verify what businesses report. Forms such as 1099s, W-2s, sales-tax reports, platform income disclosures, and foreign transaction filings all feed into massive government data-matching systems. AI ensures that every form you issue matches what your systems recorded and what your vendors and platforms are reporting. This dramatically reduces the chance of discrepancy-driven audits and protects your reputation with regulators and financial institutions.

Beyond tax filings, modern compliance includes corporate governance and regulatory reporting. Businesses must file annual reports, beneficial ownership information, business licenses, foreign qualifications, compliance certifications, and regulatory disclosures depending on industry and location. AI platforms centralize this information, track changes in ownership or structure, and generate the necessary filings automatically when something changes. This is especially critical for companies that operate multiple entities, use holding companies, or engage in complex tax strategies, because a single outdated filing can invalidate legal protections or tax elections.

For growing companies, compliance is directly tied to financing, valuation, and exit potential. Investors, lenders, and acquirers now conduct deep digital due diligence that examines tax filings, payroll reports, sales-tax compliance, and regulatory status across all jurisdictions. AI-driven compliance creates clean, verifiable audit trails that prove your business is properly structured, correctly reported, and legally compliant.

This not only reduces risk but increases the value of your company, because clean compliance records make businesses easier to finance, insure, and sell.

This book will show you how AI platforms integrate compliance across payroll, sales tax, income tax, regulatory filings, and financial reporting into one intelligent system. You will learn how AI identifies where you owe tax, what you must file, when it must be filed, and what data must be included. You will see how algorithms detect errors before filings are submitted, how they reconcile multi-system data, and how they generate regulator-ready reports that stand up to audits. Most importantly, you will learn how to design a compliance infrastructure that grows with your business rather than collapsing under its weight.

We will also explore how AI handles regulatory change. Tax laws, reporting requirements, and compliance rules evolve constantly. Human teams struggle to keep up, but AI systems are updated in real time as laws change, automatically adjusting calculations, forms, and workflows. This means your business stays compliant without needing constant manual research, retraining, or expensive consulting. AI becomes your permanent regulatory intelligence engine.

By the end of this book, you will understand why compliance is no longer a cost center but a competitive advantage when powered by artificial intelligence. Businesses that use AI to stay clean, accurate, and timely avoid penalties, reduce audits, lower administrative costs, and build trust with banks, investors, and regulators. In an economy where digital transparency is unavoidable, AI is not optional—it is the foundation of survival and success. Book 8 gives you the blueprint to build a compliance engine that protects your profits, your reputation, and your future while allowing you to scale without fear.

Chapter 1

The New Age of AI-Driven Business Compliance

In the digital economy, compliance is no longer something that happens once a year when tax season arrives; it is a continuous, real-time process that unfolds every time a sale is made, a payment is processed, a contractor is paid, or a customer clicks a checkout button. Every one of these actions generates regulatory data that governments, financial institutions, and reporting agencies monitor instantly. What used to be handled with quarterly reports and annual reconciliations is now tracked by automated systems that flag anomalies within seconds. This shift has made traditional compliance methods dangerously outdated. Businesses that rely on manual bookkeeping, delayed reporting, or disconnected software systems are operating blind in an environment that is fully digital, algorithmic, and unforgiving. Artificial intelligence changes this reality by transforming compliance from a slow, reactive burden into a fast, intelligent, always-on system that protects businesses while they grow.

Modern governments no longer wait for forms to be filed to understand what a company is doing. They collect data from banks, payroll providers, ecommerce platforms, payment processors, shipping companies, and digital marketplaces, combining it into detailed profiles of each business. If what you report does not match what those systems see, alarms go off. AI compliance platforms solve this problem by pulling data from the same sources that regulators use and reconciling it automatically before anything is filed. This ensures that sales figures, payroll numbers, tax withholdings, and expense reports are always aligned across all systems. When filings go out, they are not guesses or estimates; they are verified, cross-checked digital records that match reality.

One of the most powerful capabilities of AI in compliance is predictive risk management. Instead of waiting for an audit notice, AI systems analyze patterns in your financial and operational data to identify compliance risks before they become violations. They can detect when sales tax is being collected in one state but not properly remitted, when payroll taxes are drifting out of alignment with wages, or when contractor payments exceed reporting thresholds. These systems generate alerts, recommend corrective actions, and in many cases automatically prepare the necessary filings to fix the issue. This turns compliance from damage control into prevention, saving businesses massive amounts of money, time, and stress. AI also eliminates one of the most dangerous weaknesses in traditional compliance: human error. Typing mistakes, missed deadlines, incorrect classifications, and forgotten filings account for a huge percentage of penalties and audits. AI systems do not get tired, forget, or overlook small discrepancies. They follow strict rules, apply updated regulations, and execute tasks consistently. They track deadlines, generate forms, and submit reports with precision that no human team can match at scale. This allows businesses to operate with confidence, knowing their compliance engine is always running in the background.

As businesses expand across state lines and international borders, compliance becomes exponentially more complex. Each jurisdiction has its own tax rules, reporting requirements, and regulatory standards. AI systems map these obligations automatically based on where customers are located, where employees work, where inventory ships, and where revenue is generated. They calculate what taxes apply, which forms must be filed, and which agencies must receive reports. This makes it possible for even small businesses to operate globally without drowning in paperwork or risking costly mistakes.

Another major advantage of AI-driven compliance is transparency. Every action taken by the system is logged, timestamped, and documented. This creates a clean audit trail that can be shared with regulators, banks, investors, or buyers during due diligence. Instead of scrambling to reconstruct years of filings, businesses can instantly produce complete compliance records. This increases trust, lowers risk, and dramatically improves a company's ability to secure financing or execute a profitable exit.

In the new age of digital regulation, compliance is no longer optional, flexible, or forgiving. It is continuous, automated, and data-driven. Businesses that fail to adapt will face rising penalties, increasing audits, and growing operational friction. Those that adopt AI-powered compliance will operate with clarity, speed, and confidence, freeing their teams to focus on growth instead of paperwork. AI does not replace human judgment; it amplifies it by removing the noise, the errors, and the chaos from the compliance process.

As this book will demonstrate, the most successful businesses of the future will not be the ones with the best accountants or the biggest compliance departments. They will be the ones with the smartest AI systems managing their regulatory obligations automatically, accurately, and invisibly. Chapter 1 lays the foundation for understanding how this transformation is happening and why every business, regardless of size, must embrace AI-driven compliance to survive and thrive in the modern economy.

"The Filing That Never Failed"

When Elena started her digital marketing agency, she believed that good intentions and hard work were enough to stay compliant. She paid her taxes, hired a bookkeeper, and trusted her payroll provider to handle the paperwork. For years, everything seemed fine—until a single letter from a state tax agency arrived in her inbox. It claimed she owed tens of thousands of dollars in unpaid sales taxes from a state she had never even visited. Confused and terrified, Elena began a frantic search through her records, discovering that her online services had triggered tax obligations she never knew existed. Each system she used—Stripe, QuickBooks, her CRM—showed slightly different numbers, and none of them matched what the government claimed.

Days turned into weeks as Elena tried to untangle the mess. Phone calls went unanswered. Emails bounced between departments. Every new notice added penalties and interest. Her business, once thriving, was now paralyzed by fear and uncertainty. That was when a friend suggested she try an AI-powered compliance platform. Skeptical but desperate, Elena connected her accounts. Within minutes, the system mapped her sales across states, identified where tax was owed, calculated the correct amounts, and generated the missing filings. It even prepared letters to the tax agency explaining the discrepancies and providing corrected reports.

For the first time since the nightmare began, Elena felt a sense of control. The AI showed her exactly how the problem happened: her platform had collected tax in some states but not remitted it, while in others it failed to collect at all. The system created a step-by-step plan to bring her business back into compliance, including payment schedules and penalty abatement requests. Instead of guessing, she now had clarity.

Months later, Elena's agency was not only back on track—it was stronger than ever. Her AI compliance system monitored every transaction, filing reports automatically and alerting her to changes in tax law. When she expanded into international markets, the system handled VAT and digital service taxes without her lifting a finger. What once nearly destroyed her business had become a source of confidence and stability.

When Elena later sold a minority stake in her company to an investor, the due diligence process was effortless. Every filing, report, and compliance record was available in a clean digital archive. The investor was impressed not just by her revenue, but by the precision of her operations. Elena realized that compliance was no longer something to fear. With AI, it had become a silent partner, protecting her business and empowering her growth.

Chapter 2

Automating Every Government Filing With AI

In the past, government filings were treated as isolated events—forms prepared at the end of the month, the quarter, or the year, often rushed, error-prone, and dependent on scattered data sources. Payroll reports, sales tax returns, income tax filings, contractor disclosures, and regulatory reports all lived in different systems and were handled by different people, each working with partial information. This fragmented approach is the reason so many businesses fall out of compliance without realizing it. Artificial intelligence replaces this broken model with a unified filing engine that continuously prepares, validates, and submits every required report as part of one intelligent workflow, turning compliance into an automated background process rather than a disruptive crisis.

AI-driven filing systems begin by building a complete map of a company's obligations. They analyze where the business operates, where customers are located, where revenue is generated, where employees and contractors work, and what licenses or registrations exist. From this, the system determines exactly which forms must be filed, with which agencies, and on what schedule. This includes federal income taxes, state and local returns, sales and use tax filings, payroll tax reports, information returns like 1099s and W-2s, business license renewals, franchise taxes, and industry-specific regulatory reports. Instead of relying on memory or manual calendars, AI keeps an always-updated filing matrix that evolves as the business changes.

Once the obligation map is built, AI connects directly to the data sources that feed those filings. It pulls transactions from accounting software, payment processors, ecommerce platforms, payroll systems, and banking records, reconciling them in real time. This means the numbers used in government forms are not estimates created weeks after the fact, but precise figures derived from live financial activity. If discrepancies appear between systems, the AI flags them immediately, allowing corrections before any filing is submitted. This pre-filing validation dramatically reduces the risk of audits and penalties caused by mismatched data.

One of the greatest strengths of AI filing systems is their ability to operate continuously. Instead of waiting until the end of a reporting period, AI prepares filings incrementally as transactions occur. By the time a deadline arrives, the forms are already complete, verified, and ready for submission. In many cases, the system can file them automatically through government APIs or approved electronic filing channels. This eliminates the last-minute scrambles that plague traditional compliance teams and ensures that no deadline is ever missed.

AI also adapts instantly to changes in tax law and reporting rules. When a government agency updates a form, changes a threshold, or introduces a new filing requirement, the AI system incorporates the update into its workflows automatically. Calculations, classifications, and submission formats are adjusted without the business needing to retrain staff or hire consultants. This dynamic compliance capability is especially critical for businesses operating in multiple jurisdictions, where rules change frequently and inconsistently.

Another powerful benefit of AI-driven filing is audit readiness. Every report submitted is backed by a detailed digital trail showing where each number came from, how it was calculated, and which transactions support it. If a government agency questions a filing, the business can instantly produce supporting documentation, transaction histories, and reconciliation reports. This level of transparency not only speeds up audits but often discourages them altogether, because regulators can see that the business's data is clean, consistent, and well-documented.

As businesses grow, the volume of filings increases dramatically. What starts as a handful of forms can become hundreds of reports across dozens of agencies. AI scales effortlessly, handling this complexity without adding staff or increasing error rates. Whether a company has one employee or ten thousand, one state or fifty, one entity or a complex corporate structure, the AI filing engine maintains accuracy, consistency, and timeliness.

By automating every government filing, businesses free themselves from one of the most expensive and stressful aspects of operations. Instead of fearing compliance, they gain control over it. AI turns regulatory reporting into a predictable, reliable system that supports growth rather than hindering it. Chapter 2 shows that when filings are automated, compliance stops being a burden and becomes an invisible foundation of a strong, scalable enterprise.

"The Company That Never Missed a Deadline"

Marcus ran a fast-growing ecommerce brand that sold products in nearly every state. At first, managing compliance was manageable. But as sales exploded, so did his filing obligations. Sales tax returns, payroll reports, 1099s, franchise taxes, and license renewals piled up, each with its own deadline and agency. Despite his best efforts, Marcus missed one small filing in a state he barely did business in. The penalty was small at first, but it snowballed into late fees, interest, and eventually a frozen business account that halted his operations for days.

That scare changed everything. Marcus implemented an AI-powered filing system, connecting it to his store, payroll, and accounting software. Within hours, the system built a complete map of his obligations across all states. It showed him dozens of filings he never even knew existed. More importantly, it began preparing them automatically, reconciling data as orders came in and payments were processed.

The first month with the AI felt surreal. Instead of chasing deadlines, Marcus received notifications that filings had already been completed and submitted. Sales tax returns were sent to the right states. Payroll reports were filed on time. Contractor forms were generated and delivered without him lifting a finger. When one state updated its sales tax rules, the AI adjusted automatically.

A year later, Marcus's business had tripled in size, but his compliance workload had dropped to almost zero. When his bank requested proof of tax compliance for a line of credit, Marcus sent a single link to his AI compliance dashboard. The bank approved the loan in days. What once felt like a constant threat had become one of his company's greatest strengths. His business no longer worried about missing deadlines—because it never did.

Chapter 3

Real-Time Compliance Monitoring & Risk Prevention With AI

In the traditional compliance model, businesses discover problems only after damage has already been done. A late filing notice arrives. A penalty hits the bank account. An audit letter appears in the mail. By the time anyone reacts, the system has already recorded a failure. Artificial intelligence completely reverses this pattern by turning compliance into a real-time monitoring system that watches every financial, payroll, tax, and reporting activity as it happens. Instead of waiting for mistakes to surface, AI detects risk the moment it begins forming and intervenes before a violation ever occurs. This shift—from reaction to prevention—is one of the most powerful transformations AI brings to modern business compliance.

Every transaction a business makes carries regulatory implications. A sale may create sales tax liability in a new state. A payment to a contractor may trigger information reporting. A payroll run may change employment tax obligations. A new customer in a foreign country may activate VAT or digital services tax requirements. AI systems continuously analyze this stream of activity, matching it against current laws and reporting thresholds. When the system sees that an obligation is being created or approached, it flags it immediately. This allows businesses to take corrective action before noncompliance becomes a legal or financial problem.

One of the most important ways AI reduces compliance risk is by detecting data inconsistencies across systems. Governments compare what businesses report to what banks, payment processors, and platforms report about them. Even small mismatches can trigger audits. AI compliance platforms continuously reconcile data between accounting software, payroll systems, ecommerce platforms, and bank feeds. If one system shows more revenue than another, or if tax collected does not match tax reported, the AI highlights the discrepancy and recommends fixes. This prevents the silent accumulation of errors that so often lead to painful enforcement actions.

AI also monitors filing status and regulatory health in real time. It tracks whether forms have been prepared, reviewed, submitted, accepted, or rejected. If a filing fails or is delayed, the system escalates the issue instantly. Instead of discovering weeks later that a form was never processed, businesses know within minutes and can correct the problem. This kind of live oversight is impossible with manual processes, but it is routine for AI-driven compliance engines. Another critical function of

AI risk prevention is anomaly detection. The system learns what normal activity looks like for a business—typical sales volumes, payroll levels, expense patterns, and tax rates. When something unusual occurs, such as a sudden spike in revenue in a new state, an unexpected drop in payroll taxes, or a classification error, the AI flags it for review. These anomalies are often the early warning signs of compliance issues, fraud, or operational mistakes. Catching them early saves businesses from far more serious consequences later.

AI also plays a major role in regulatory intelligence. Laws and reporting rules change constantly, and businesses often fail to update their processes fast enough. AI systems receive continuous updates from tax authorities and regulatory bodies, adjusting calculations, thresholds, and filing rules in real time. This ensures that compliance monitoring is always based on the latest law, not outdated assumptions. Businesses no longer need to worry about missing a change that could put them out of compliance overnight.

The result of real-time compliance monitoring is peace of mind. Instead of fearing audits, penalties, and regulatory surprises, businesses operate with confidence, knowing that their AI system is watching everything and keeping them within the rules. Problems are addressed while they are still small, before they become expensive or dangerous. This is the true power of AI in compliance—not just automation, but intelligent, continuous protection.

Chapter 3 shows that in a world where governments use data and algorithms to enforce compliance, businesses must do the same to protect themselves. Real-time AI monitoring creates a protective shield around every transaction, every filing, and every report. It turns compliance into a living system that adapts, corrects, and defends your business as it grows.

"The Alert That Saved the Company"

Sophia owned a fast-scaling software startup that sold subscriptions to customers around the world. Everything was running smoothly until one afternoon her AI compliance system sent an urgent alert. It had detected that her company was collecting payments from customers in a European country without charging the required digital services tax. The amount was small at first, but the system projected that within weeks it would exceed the reporting threshold and trigger penalties.

Sophia was stunned. Her accounting team had no idea the tax applied. Without the AI, the problem would have gone unnoticed for months. The system had already calculated the correct tax rate, generated the necessary registrations, and prepared the filings. All Sophia had to do was approve the action.

Within hours, her company was properly registered, tax collection was enabled, and the risk was gone. A potential compliance disaster had been eliminated before it ever reached a regulator's radar. Weeks later, when she learned that several competitors had been fined for the same mistake, Sophia realized how close she had come to serious trouble.

From that day on, she trusted her AI compliance system more than any checklist or manual review. It watched her business around the clock, catching risks she would never have seen. What once felt like a fragile, vulnerable operation now felt protected and resilient. All because one alert arrived at exactly the right moment.

Chapter 4

Building a Fully Autonomous Compliance Infrastructure With AI

For most businesses, compliance is not broken because people are careless; it is broken because the system itself was never designed to scale. As companies grow, add revenue streams, expand into new jurisdictions, hire employees, engage contractors, sell online, and integrate multiple platforms, compliance requirements multiply faster than human teams can realistically manage. Each new activity creates new filings, new reporting rules, new deadlines, and new risks. What once required a simple checklist becomes a constantly shifting maze. Artificial intelligence allows businesses to escape this trap by building a fully autonomous compliance infrastructure—one that operates continuously, adapts automatically, and scales without friction.

An autonomous compliance infrastructure is not a single tool or piece of software; it is an ecosystem. At its core is an AI engine that connects accounting, payroll, banking, ecommerce, invoicing, expense tracking, and tax systems into one unified compliance brain. This engine understands not just transactions, but intent and structure. It knows why money moved, how it should be classified, where it must be reported, and which agencies must receive it. Instead of compliance being layered on top of operations, it becomes embedded directly into the way the business functions.

The first step in building autonomy is eliminating manual handoffs. Traditional compliance depends on humans moving data from one system to another—exporting reports, copying numbers, uploading files, checking boxes. Every handoff introduces delay and error. AI removes these handoffs by synchronizing systems automatically. Transactions flow seamlessly from operational platforms into compliance workflows. Classifications happen instantly. Reporting thresholds are monitored in real time. Filing preparation becomes a background process rather than a scheduled event.

The second step is decision automation. Many compliance failures occur not because businesses do nothing, but because they make the wrong decision too late. Should this contractor be classified as an employee? Does this sale trigger nexus in a new state? Is this transaction subject to withholding or reporting? AI systems are trained on regulatory rules and historical enforcement patterns, allowing them to make these decisions consistently and immediately. When human review is required, the system flags the decision early, before a violation occurs. Autonomous compliance systems also manage regulatory identity. Businesses are not static entities;

they evolve. Ownership changes, entities are formed or dissolved, elections are made, licenses are added or expire. AI tracks these changes and ensures that government records reflect reality. When an ownership percentage shifts, the system updates beneficial ownership filings. When a new entity is created, it registers it with the appropriate agencies. When a license renewal is due, it prepares and submits the application automatically. This prevents one of the most common compliance breakdowns: outdated or inaccurate government records.

Another critical element of autonomy is self-correction. AI systems do not just detect problems; they fix them. If a filing is rejected, the system analyzes the reason, corrects the issue, and resubmits. If a discrepancy appears between systems, the AI reconciles it or escalates it for review. If a regulation changes, workflows are updated automatically. This creates a compliance infrastructure that improves over time instead of degrading as complexity increases.

Autonomy also transforms compliance economics. Traditionally, growing compliance requires hiring more staff, engaging more consultants, and paying more fees. AI breaks this linear relationship. Once the infrastructure is built, it can handle ten times—or one hundred times—the volume with minimal additional cost. This gives businesses a structural advantage over competitors who are still trapped in manual processes. Compliance stops being a bottleneck and becomes a silent enabler of growth.

Most importantly, a fully autonomous compliance infrastructure changes how leaders think. Instead of asking, "Are we compliant?" they begin to assume compliance as a given. Attention shifts from fear and damage control to strategy, expansion, and innovation. AI does not remove responsibility from business owners; it gives them a system that executes responsibility flawlessly. Chapter 4 demonstrates that autonomy is not the future of compliance—it is the only sustainable way to operate in a world of continuous digital regulation.

"The Business That Ran Itself"

When Daniel launched his first company, compliance was something he dealt with late at night, long after the real work was done. He remembered missed deadlines, confusing notices, and the constant anxiety that something important had slipped through the cracks. Years later, when he founded a new venture—a multi-entity, multi-state online services business—he promised himself it would be different. From day one, he built the company around an AI-driven compliance infrastructure.

At first, the system felt excessive. It tracked every transaction, every payroll run, every invoice, every regulatory obligation. But as the business grew, Daniel noticed something strange: compliance never became harder. New states were added automatically. New filings appeared on the dashboard without him asking. When the company hired its first international contractor, the system flagged the reporting requirements and handled the registration process before Daniel even understood what was required.

Months turned into years, and the company expanded rapidly. Competitors struggled with audits, frozen accounts, and compliance fires that pulled founders away from growth. Daniel watched from a distance, almost detached. His AI system handled filings, corrected errors, and adapted to law changes without drama. When a filing was rejected, it was fixed and resubmitted before Daniel ever saw the notification.

One day, during a board meeting, an investor asked a simple question: "Who handles compliance?" Daniel smiled and pointed to the dashboard. Every filing, every report, every approval was visible in real time. The investor was stunned. During due diligence, regulators requested documentation covering multiple years and jurisdictions. Daniel delivered everything in minutes. There were no gaps, no inconsistencies, no panic. As the company prepared for acquisition, the buyer's legal team expected weeks of compliance review. Instead, they found a business that seemed to run itself. The AI compliance infrastructure had eliminated uncertainty, reduced risk, and created absolute operational clarity. When the deal closed at a premium valuation, Daniel realized something profound: the greatest asset he had built was not the product or the revenue—it was a system that made compliance invisible, automatic, and flawless.

Chapter 5

Turning Compliance Into a Strategic Advantage With AI

For most businesses, compliance has always been viewed as a necessary evil—an unavoidable cost of doing business that produces no direct revenue and offers little visible return. Taxes must be filed, reports must be submitted, licenses must be renewed, and regulations must be followed, regardless of whether a company is profitable or struggling. This mindset has conditioned business owners to see compliance as something to minimize, outsource, or delay rather than something to design intentionally. Artificial intelligence fundamentally changes this equation by transforming compliance from a passive obligation into an active strategic advantage that strengthens profitability, stability, and long-term enterprise value.

The moment compliance becomes automated, accurate, and continuous, it stops being reactive and starts becoming informative. AI-powered compliance systems do not merely ensure that rules are followed; they generate insights about how the business operates within regulatory frameworks. They reveal where taxes are being overpaid, where registrations are unnecessary, where entity structures are inefficient, and where reporting choices impact cash flow. Instead of compliance draining resources, it begins to illuminate opportunities for optimization and smarter decision-making.

One of the most powerful strategic benefits of AI-driven compliance is financial predictability. When filings are automated and monitored in real time, businesses gain clear visibility into upcoming tax liabilities, regulatory costs, and cash outflows. AI systems forecast obligations weeks or months in advance, allowing leaders to plan distributions, investments, hiring, and expansion without fear of surprise liabilities. This level of certainty is nearly impossible to achieve with manual systems, where numbers are reconciled late and obligations are discovered after the fact.

AI also enables proactive regulatory positioning. Businesses that understand their compliance posture in real time can make strategic moves before rules become restrictive or costly. For example, AI can model how expanding into a new state or country will affect tax exposure, reporting obligations, and compliance costs before the expansion occurs. It can simulate different entity structures, payroll configurations, or sales models and show how each impacts regulatory burden. This allows leaders to design growth strategies that maximize profit while minimizing friction. Another critical advantage of AI-powered compliance is credibility. In today's economy, trust is currency. Banks, investors, insurers, partners, and acquirers all assess compliance quality as a proxy for operational maturity. Companies with clean, consistent, AI-verified compliance records are seen as lower risk and higher quality. They receive better financing terms, higher valuations, and smoother approvals. AI compliance systems produce audit-ready documentation by default, making trust scalable rather than dependent on personal relationships or last-minute cleanup efforts.

Compliance automation also protects leadership focus. Every hour spent dealing with penalties, audits, notices, and corrections is an hour not spent building products, serving customers, or creating value. AI removes this distraction entirely. When compliance runs autonomously, founders and executives are freed from constant vigilance and anxiety. This mental clarity is itself a strategic advantage, allowing leaders to operate decisively and confidently rather than defensively.

Perhaps most importantly, AI reframes compliance as a defensive moat. Businesses that rely on manual or fragmented systems are vulnerable to enforcement actions, regulatory changes, and scaling failures. Those vulnerabilities compound over time, especially as operations become more complex. An AI-driven compliance infrastructure, by contrast, becomes stronger as the business grows. It adapts, learns, and scales, creating a barrier that competitors struggle to replicate. In highly regulated industries or competitive markets, this can be the difference between sustained success and sudden collapse.

By turning compliance into a strategic asset rather than a liability, AI reshapes the entire relationship between businesses and regulation. Instead of fearing oversight, companies leverage clarity. Instead of hiding from rules, they design around them intelligently. Chapter 5 shows that when compliance is automated, transparent, and intelligent, it becomes one of the most powerful tools a business can use to protect profits, enable growth, and increase long-term value.

"The Quiet Advantage"

No one in the industry understood why Olivia's company always seemed to move faster, raise capital more easily, and survive disruptions that crippled others. On the surface, her business looked similar to dozens of competitors—same market, same pricing, similar products. But beneath the surface, there was something fundamentally different. While others treated compliance as an afterthought, Olivia had built her company around an AI-driven compliance core from the very beginning.

In the early days, when revenue was modest and operations were simple, some advisors told her the system was unnecessary. "You can worry about compliance later," they said. Olivia ignored them. She had seen too many businesses collapse under the weight of penalties, audits, and regulatory chaos. She wanted certainty, not luck. So she connected every system—banking, accounting, payroll, sales platforms—into an AI compliance engine that tracked everything in real time.

As the company grew, that decision quietly began to pay off. When competitors expanded into new states, they stumbled into unexpected tax obligations and reporting failures. Olivia's AI system, by contrast, modeled the expansion in advance, registering the business, adjusting tax collection, and preparing filings before the first sale was ever made. While others reacted to problems, Olivia avoided them entirely.

The real difference became visible during a market downturn. Cash tightened, investors grew cautious, and regulators increased scrutiny. Several competitors received audit notices and faced frozen accounts at the worst possible moment. Olivia's company received none. Her filings were clean, her data matched across systems, and her compliance history showed years of consistency. Banks extended credit. Investors leaned in. While others scrambled to survive, Olivia continued to grow.

During a major funding round, due diligence teams expected

weeks of back-and-forth requests. Instead, Olivia provided instant access to a complete compliance dashboard—every filing, every report, every confirmation neatly organized and verifiable. The investors were stunned. One of them said quietly, "This is one of the cleanest operations we've ever seen." The valuation reflected that confidence.

Years later, when Olivia sold the company at a premium, journalists focused on her product and market timing. They missed the real story. The quiet advantage was never visible from the outside. It lived in the systems, the automation, the absence of chaos. While others fought fires, Olivia built value. AI compliance didn't just protect her business—it gave her an edge no one else could see until it was too late.

Chapter 6

Future-Proofing Your Business Against Regulatory Change With AI

One of the most underestimated threats to modern businesses is not competition, technology, or even economic cycles—it is regulatory change. Laws evolve constantly, often quietly, and usually faster than human teams can adapt. New reporting requirements appear with little warning. Thresholds shift. Definitions change. Entire filing regimes are introduced seemingly overnight. For businesses relying on manual compliance processes, each regulatory change introduces risk, confusion, and delay. Artificial intelligence fundamentally alters this dynamic by giving businesses the ability to anticipate, absorb, and adapt to regulatory change automatically, turning uncertainty into a manageable—and even strategic—component of long-term planning.

Traditional compliance systems are static by nature. They are built around current rules, documented procedures, and human knowledge that quickly becomes outdated. When regulations change, businesses must retrain staff, update checklists, revise workflows, and often correct mistakes made during the transition. This lag is where most compliance failures occur. AI systems, by contrast, are designed for continuous learning. They ingest updates from tax authorities, regulatory agencies, and legal databases in real time, adjusting calculations, classifications, and filing requirements automatically. This ensures that compliance processes remain aligned with the latest rules without requiring constant manual intervention.

Future-proofing with AI begins with regulatory intelligence. Advanced compliance systems do not simply react to rule changes; they monitor regulatory signals across jurisdictions. Proposed laws, draft regulations, enforcement trends, and agency guidance are analyzed to predict how compliance obligations may shift. AI models identify patterns in enforcement behavior, highlighting areas where regulators are increasing scrutiny. This allows businesses to prepare for change before it becomes mandatory, adjusting structures, processes, or reporting strategies proactively rather than defensively.

Another critical aspect of future-proofing is flexibility. Businesses evolve continuously—new products, new markets, new revenue models. Each change interacts with regulation in complex ways. AI compliance systems simulate the regulatory impact of strategic decisions before they are executed. Leaders can model how entering a new state affects sales tax exposure, how changing pricing structures impacts reporting, or how hiring remote employees alters payroll obligations. This scenario planning capability transforms compliance from a constraint into a design variable that can be optimized alongside growth.

AI also future-proofs businesses by creating resilience against enforcement shocks. Regulatory crackdowns rarely affect everyone equally. They tend to expose weak systems, inconsistent data, and outdated processes. Businesses with AI-driven compliance infrastructures are insulated from these shocks because their data is clean, reconciled, and continuously verified. When regulators tighten rules or expand audits, AI-equipped businesses already meet the new standards. Instead of scrambling to respond, they continue operating normally while competitors struggle.

Perhaps most importantly, AI future-proofs leadership decision-making. When compliance is uncertain, leaders hesitate. Expansion is delayed. Opportunities are avoided. Risk aversion replaces innovation. AI removes this fear by providing real-time visibility into regulatory exposure. Leaders know where they stand, what is changing, and what actions are required. This confidence enables decisive action even in volatile regulatory environments, giving AI-powered businesses a long-term strategic advantage. Future-proofing is not about predicting every rule that will ever exist. It is about building systems that adapt faster than change itself. AI does exactly that. It absorbs complexity, translates regulation into executable logic, and evolves alongside the business. Chapter 6 demonstrates that in a world of accelerating regulation, the only sustainable strategy is automation, intelligence, and adaptability. AI does not eliminate regulation—but it ensures regulation never becomes a threat to your future.

"The Rule That Changed Everything"

When the announcement came, it arrived quietly—just another update buried in a regulatory bulletin most business owners never read. A new reporting requirement, effective in ninety days, expanded disclosure obligations for companies operating across multiple jurisdictions. The penalties for noncompliance were severe, and enforcement would begin immediately. Within weeks, panic spread across the industry. Advisors scrambled. Compliance teams worked overtime. Businesses realized too late that their systems were unprepared for the change.

Ethan heard about the rule not from the news, but from his AI compliance system. One morning, he opened his dashboard to find a notice labeled "Upcoming Regulatory Impact." The system had already analyzed the new rule, mapped it against his operations, and identified exactly which entities, transactions, and reports would be affected. It projected the compliance workload, updated filing schedules, and recommended structural adjustments—all before Ethan had fully understood what the rule even meant.

As the deadline approached, competitors struggled. Some misunderstood the requirements. Others submitted incomplete reports. Many missed deadlines entirely. Notices, penalties, and audits followed. Entire finance teams were pulled into emergency response mode. Ethan watched from a distance, almost uncomfortable with how calm everything felt. His AI system had already updated data flows, modified classifications, and prepared the new filings automatically. When the rule went into effect, his company was already compliant.

Months later, regulators announced expanded enforcement and retroactive reviews. Businesses that had rushed to comply discovered errors in their submissions. Ethan's company was reviewed as well—but the audit lasted less than a day. Every report matched underlying data perfectly. Every obligation was documented. The auditors moved on quickly, leaving behind nothing but a confirmation letter.

The true impact of the rule became clear a year later. Several competitors exited the market, unable to recover from penalties and compliance costs. Ethan's company, by contrast, had grown. While others diverted resources to survival, he invested in expansion. When asked how he navigated the regulatory upheaval so smoothly, Ethan gave a simple answer: he didn't react to change—his systems adapted to it automatically.

Looking back, Ethan realized the rule itself was never the real challenge. The challenge was speed. In a world where regulation moves faster than humans can respond, only intelligent systems can keep up. His AI compliance infrastructure didn't just protect his business—it allowed it to thrive while others fell behind.

Chapter 7

Scaling Compliance Without Limits: How AI Grows With Your Business

Growth is often celebrated as the ultimate sign of business success, yet it is also the moment when compliance systems begin to fracture. What works for a small operation quickly collapses under the weight of expansion. New revenue streams introduce new reporting rules. New locations create new tax jurisdictions. New employees, contractors, partners, and platforms multiply filing obligations. For businesses relying on manual processes or fragmented tools, growth becomes dangerous rather than empowering. Artificial intelligence solves this paradox by enabling compliance to scale infinitely, automatically, and proportionally—without increasing complexity, cost, or risk.

Traditional compliance scales linearly. More revenue means more transactions. More transactions mean more reports. More reports mean more staff, more consultants, and more opportunities for error. This model eventually breaks, because human systems cannot process exponential complexity without failure. AI replaces linear scaling with exponential efficiency. Once an AI-driven compliance infrastructure is in place, it does not matter whether a business processes one hundred transactions or one million. The system applies the same rules, the same validations, and the same reporting logic instantly and consistently.

At the core of scalable compliance is abstraction. AI systems do not manage individual forms in isolation; they manage compliance logic. They understand how rules apply across scenarios and jurisdictions. When a business enters a new market, adds a new product line, or launches a new entity, the AI does not start from zero. It extends existing logic, mapping new activity into established compliance frameworks. This allows businesses to grow without rebuilding processes each time something changes.

AI also scales compliance visibility. As organizations grow, leadership often loses sight of compliance status. Information becomes siloed across departments, entities, and geographies. AI centralizes compliance intelligence into a single, unified view. Leaders can see filing status, regulatory exposure, upcoming obligations, and risk indicators across the entire organization in real time. This clarity is essential for large or fast-growing businesses, where even small blind spots can lead to major consequences.

Another key factor in scalability is consistency. In growing organizations, compliance failures often stem from inconsistency—different teams interpreting rules differently, using different data sources, or following outdated procedures. AI enforces uniform standards across the entire business. Every transaction is classified the same way. Every filing is prepared using the same logic. Every jurisdiction is handled according to the latest rules. This eliminates internal variation and ensures that compliance quality does not degrade as the organization expands.

AI also enables compliance delegation without loss of control. As businesses grow, responsibilities must be distributed across teams, departments, or regions. AI systems allow tasks to be delegated while maintaining centralized oversight. Permissions, workflows, and approvals are managed within the system, ensuring accountability without chaos. This allows organizations to scale operationally without sacrificing governance.

Perhaps the most overlooked aspect of scalable compliance is sustainability. Growth often leads to burnout, especially among finance and compliance teams overwhelmed by increasing demands. AI removes this pressure by absorbing complexity and repetition. Teams shift from firefighting to oversight and strategy. Instead of reacting to problems, they monitor systems that work reliably in the background. This not only improves compliance outcomes but also strengthens organizational culture and retention.

Scaling without limits is not about ignoring regulation; it is about mastering it through systems designed for growth. AI makes compliance elastic, resilient, and invisible, even as complexity increases. Chapter 7 shows that businesses no longer need to choose between growth and control. With AI, they can have both—expanding confidently while maintaining perfect regulatory alignment at every stage of scale.

"The Company That Outgrew the Chaos"

When the company was small, compliance felt manageable. A few filings, a handful of deadlines, and the occasional reminder from an accountant were enough to keep things running smoothly. But as the business grew, chaos crept in quietly. New customers came from new states. New contractors joined from different countries. Revenue streams multiplied. Each expansion felt exciting—until the compliance questions started piling up. What applied where? Who was responsible? What had already been filed? No one seemed to have a complete answer.

Maya watched this happen at her first startup. Growth was explosive, but compliance lagged behind. Filings were missed. Notices arrived. Accounts were temporarily frozen. Entire weeks were lost to damage control. When the company finally stabilized, it was too late. The opportunity had passed. Years later, when Maya launched her own venture, she made one decision that changed everything: compliance would scale before growth did.

From day one, she implemented an AI-driven compliance system designed not just to handle current needs, but to absorb future complexity. At first, the system felt oversized. It tracked jurisdictions she didn't yet operate in and monitored thresholds she hadn't reached. But Maya understood something others didn't—growth doesn't ask permission. When it comes, systems must already be ready.

The first real test came sooner than expected. A viral partnership tripled revenue in a matter of months. Orders flooded in from states the company had never sold to before. Competitors in the same space struggled immediately. Some stopped accepting orders from certain regions. Others paused growth to "figure out compliance." Maya did neither. Her AI system detected new nexus points automatically, registered the business where required, adjusted tax collection, and prepared filings without disruption. Customers never noticed. Growth continued uninterrupted.

As the company expanded internationally, the pattern repeated. While others hesitated, Maya moved forward confidently. The AI system mapped each new country's requirements, calculated obligations, and integrated reporting seamlessly. There were no emergency meetings, no frantic emails, no last-minute fixes. Compliance simply happened, invisibly, as part of operations.

Years later, the company was no longer a startup—it was a complex, multi-entity organization operating at scale. New hires were often surprised by how calm everything felt. There were no compliance fire drills, no looming deadlines dominating conversations. Instead, there was clarity. Dashboards showed real-time status. Alerts arrived before issues formed. Leadership meetings focused on strategy, not survival.

When analysts later studied Maya's company to understand its success, they pointed to product-market fit, timing, and execution. They missed the real story. The true differentiator was structural. Maya had built a business that could grow without breaking because compliance was never an afterthought. It was a system designed to scale faster than chaos itself—and that made all the difference.

Chapter 8

Achieving Total Transparency, Audit Readiness & Long-Term Trust With AI

In the modern regulatory environment, transparency is no longer optional. Governments, financial institutions, investors, and partners all expect businesses to produce clean, consistent, and verifiable records on demand. The era of "close enough" reporting is over. Today, data is compared across multiple sources automatically, and inconsistencies are treated as red flags rather than minor mistakes. Artificial intelligence fundamentally reshapes this landscape by making total transparency and perpetual audit readiness the default state of a business, rather than a stressful, last-minute effort triggered by an inquiry or enforcement action.

Traditional audit preparation is reactive. Businesses scramble when an audit notice arrives, pulling records from multiple systems, reconciling numbers retroactively, and attempting to explain discrepancies after the fact. This approach is costly, disruptive, and risky. AI-driven compliance replaces this model with continuous audit readiness. Every transaction is recorded, classified, reconciled, and documented in real time. Supporting evidence is attached automatically. Calculations are logged. Decisions are traceable. When an audit occurs, there is no preparation phase—only presentation.

AI achieves this by creating a single source of truth across all financial and regulatory data. Accounting records, payroll data, tax filings, sales reports, banking transactions, and regulatory submissions are synchronized continuously. Each number reported to a government agency can be traced back to its origin with full context. This level of traceability eliminates ambiguity, which is the primary driver of prolonged audits and disputes. Regulators are far less likely to challenge filings when the data is clear, consistent, and easily verifiable.

Transparency also changes the tone of regulatory interactions. Businesses that rely on manual systems often approach audits defensively, fearing that errors will be discovered. AI-powered businesses approach audits confidently, knowing that their records are accurate and complete. This confidence is not psychological—it is structural. The system itself enforces consistency and completeness, removing the uncertainty that makes audits adversarial.

Beyond audits, transparency is critical for internal governance. As organizations grow, leaders need visibility into compliance health across entities, regions, and departments. AI dashboards provide real-time insight into filing status, regulatory exposure, historical compliance performance, and risk indicators. This allows executives and boards to fulfill fiduciary duties effectively, making informed decisions based on accurate, current information rather than delayed reports.

AI-driven transparency also strengthens external trust. Banks use compliance history to assess lending risk. Investors examine filings and regulatory posture during due diligence. Acquirers evaluate audit trails to determine valuation and deal structure. Businesses with AI-verified compliance records move through these processes faster and with less friction. Trust becomes scalable, no longer dependent on individual explanations or manual documentation.

Another critical benefit of transparency is dispute prevention and resolution. When disagreements arise—whether with tax authorities, regulators, or partners—AI-backed records provide objective evidence. Dates, amounts, classifications, and filings are documented clearly. This reduces subjective interpretation and accelerates resolution. In many cases, disputes are avoided entirely because the data speaks for itself.

Ultimately, transparency is about longevity. Businesses that survive decades do so because they earn and maintain trust—not just with customers, but with institutions. AI embeds transparency into the DNA of operations, ensuring that trust is not something earned repeatedly through effort, but something maintained automatically through systems. Chapter 8 shows that total transparency is no longer a burden. With AI, it is the natural outcome of doing business the right way.

"Nothing to Hide"

The audit notice arrived on a Tuesday morning, quietly, without urgency or drama. For most business owners, that single message would have triggered panic. Meetings would be canceled. Teams would be pulled into emergency mode. Emails would fly as records were hastily gathered. But for Aaron, the moment passed almost unnoticed.

He had built his company during a time when compliance horror stories were common. Friends had lost months of productivity responding to audits. Some had paid penalties not because they were dishonest, but because they couldn't prove they were right. Aaron decided early on that he would never run a business that depended on memory, spreadsheets, or last-minute explanations. From the beginning, he invested in an AI-driven compliance system designed around transparency.

Every transaction in Aaron's company told a story. When money moved, the system recorded not just the amount, but the purpose, the source, the destination, and the regulatory implication. Sales were linked to invoices, invoices to payments, payments to bank records, and bank records to tax filings. Payroll runs connected automatically to employment reports. Every filing included embedded documentation showing exactly how each number was calculated.

So when the audit notice arrived, Aaron didn't scramble. He opened his dashboard, selected the audit period, and granted the auditors read-only access to the relevant records. Within minutes, they could see everything—every filing, every confirmation, every reconciliation. There were no missing documents, no unexplained variances, no handwritten notes trying to reconstruct the past.

Days passed. Then weeks. Aaron heard almost nothing. While other founders swapped horror stories online, he continued running his business as usual. The audit, it turned out, was routine. The auditors had selected his company at random, expecting the usual back-and-forth. Instead, they found a system where every answer was already visible.

When questions did arise, they were resolved instantly. A flagged transaction? Clicked and explained. A reported amount? Traced directly to its source. A filing date? Verified with digital confirmation. The auditors didn't argue—they confirmed. The audit closed without adjustment. No penalties.

No changes. No follow-up. Just a short message thanking the company for its cooperation and clarity.

Months later, Aaron found himself in a different kind of review—due diligence for a major acquisition. This time, the scrutiny was even deeper. Legal teams examined years of records across multiple jurisdictions. Again, the system did the work. Transparency wasn't something Aaron had to defend; it was something buyers could see for themselves.

When the deal closed at a premium valuation, one of the acquiring executives said something Aaron never forgot: "There was nothing to question." That was the moment he fully understood the power of AI-driven transparency. It didn't just protect his business—it removed doubt entirely. In a world where suspicion is common and proof is everything, Aaron's company had nothing to hide, and everything to gain.

Chapter 9

Compliance as a Valuation Engine: How AI Increases Business Worth

For most entrepreneurs, valuation is discussed in terms of revenue, profit, growth rate, and market opportunity. Rarely does compliance appear on that list, yet in reality, compliance quality is one of the strongest hidden drivers of business value. Investors, lenders, and acquirers do not simply buy earnings; they buy certainty. They assess risk, stability, and predictability as much as they assess upside. Artificial intelligence transforms compliance into a valuation engine by removing uncertainty, strengthening trust, and proving that a business can operate cleanly, efficiently, and sustainably at scale.

In traditional businesses, compliance is often fragmented and opaque. Records are scattered across systems. Filings depend on individual employees or external accountants. Historical data is difficult to reconstruct. During due diligence, these weaknesses surface quickly. Questions multiply. Timelines stretch. Deals are repriced or abandoned altogether. Even profitable companies lose value because buyers factor in the cost and risk of fixing compliance issues after acquisition.

AI-driven compliance eliminates this discount by making regulatory clarity visible, verifiable, and continuous.

One of the most powerful ways AI increases valuation is through audit-grade financial integrity. Every number reported by an AI-enabled business is traceable back to source data. Revenue aligns with bank deposits. Expenses match invoices. Payroll reports reconcile perfectly with tax filings. Sales tax, VAT, and income tax obligations are calculated consistently across jurisdictions. This alignment signals operational maturity. Buyers and investors interpret it as evidence that earnings are real, repeatable, and defensible.

AI also increases valuation by accelerating due diligence. In acquisitions, time kills deals. The longer due diligence drags on, the more opportunities there are for doubt, renegotiation, or deal fatigue. AI compliance platforms compress months of document requests into hours. Instead of manually responding to questionnaires and assembling records, businesses grant controlled access to compliance dashboards that show filing history, confirmations, audit trails, and regulatory status in real time. This speed reduces friction and preserves deal momentum, often resulting in better terms.

Another valuation multiplier created by AI compliance is scalability assurance. Buyers are not only interested in what a business is today, but in what it can become. A company that requires manual compliance processes is expensive to scale and fragile under growth. A company with AI-driven compliance demonstrates that it can expand into new markets, add revenue streams, and increase transaction volume without proportional increases in risk or overhead. This makes future growth more credible, which directly impacts valuation models.

AI also protects valuation by preventing negative surprises. Nothing destroys deal value faster than undisclosed compliance issues discovered late in the process. Back taxes, missed filings, unresolved audits, or regulatory exposure force buyers to demand price reductions, escrow holdbacks, or indemnities. AI minimizes this risk by ensuring that issues are identified and resolved continuously, long before a transaction occurs. By the time a business enters negotiations, its compliance posture is already clean.

Beyond transactions, AI-driven compliance increases valuation in ongoing financing and partnerships. Banks offer better lending terms to businesses with strong compliance histories. Investors are more willing to deploy capital when regulatory risk is low. Strategic partners prefer companies that operate transparently and reliably. These advantages compound over time, lowering cost of capital and increasing strategic optionality.

Ultimately, valuation is about confidence. Confidence that the numbers are accurate. Confidence that risks are controlled. Confidence that growth will not trigger regulatory failure. AI creates this confidence structurally, not rhetorically. Chapter 9 demonstrates that compliance is no longer just about avoiding penalties—it is about proving worth. Businesses that embed AI into compliance do not merely protect value; they manufacture it.

"The Deal That Almost Didn't Happen"

When the offer arrived, it was everything Lucas had worked toward for nearly a decade. A respected private equity firm proposed to acquire a majority stake in his company at a valuation that would change his life. The numbers made sense. Revenue was strong. Growth was consistent. The market outlook was favorable. Lucas allowed himself a moment of celebration—until due diligence began.

At first, the requests seemed routine. Tax returns, payroll reports, sales records. Lucas forwarded them confidently. Then the follow-up questions started. Why did reported revenue differ slightly from bank deposits in one quarter? Why did sales tax filings in certain states lag behind platform reports? Why were contractor payments classified differently across years? None of these issues were dramatic on their own, but together they created uncertainty. The buyer's tone shifted. Conversations slowed. New conditions appeared in the term sheet.

Lucas felt the deal slipping. He knew the business was legitimate. He had never tried to hide anything. But proving that truth across years of fragmented records was exhausting. His advisors warned him that the buyer might reduce the valuation or walk away entirely. That was when Lucas made a decision that felt risky in the moment but would later define the outcome: he paused the process and rebuilt compliance from the ground up using AI.

The implementation took weeks, not years. The AI system ingested historical data, reconciled discrepancies, corrected misclassifications, and generated clean, consistent records across all filings. It identified errors Lucas never knew existed and fixed them proactively. By the time he reengaged with the buyer, his company looked fundamentally different—not in what it did, but in how clearly it could prove it.

Lucas reopened the data room, this time granting access through an AI-powered compliance dashboard. Every filing was linked to source transactions. Every number could be traced, explained, and verified instantly. The buyer's analysts moved faster than expected. Questions that once took days to answer were resolved in minutes. The tone shifted again—this time toward confidence. Then came the moment Lucas never expected. The buyer returned with a revised offer—higher than the original. The explanation was simple: risk had been removed. What once looked like uncertainty now looked like institutional-grade operations. The firm believed the company could scale further, faster, without regulatory friction.

When the deal closed, Lucas reflected on how close he had come to losing everything he had built—not because his business was flawed, but because his compliance systems were invisible. AI had changed that. It turned complexity into clarity, suspicion into trust, and effort into proof. The deal almost didn't happen, but in the end, it became something better than Lucas had imagined. Compliance didn't just save the valuation—it increased it.

Chapter 10

The AI-First Compliance Model: Redefining How Businesses Operate Forever

The final transformation that artificial intelligence brings to compliance is not incremental—it is foundational. When businesses move from using AI as a support tool to designing operations around an AI-first compliance model, the relationship between regulation and business changes permanently. Compliance is no longer something managed alongside operations; it becomes the operating system itself. Every decision, transaction, expansion, and report flows through intelligent systems that interpret rules instantly and execute obligations automatically. This shift represents the end of reactive compliance and the beginning of a new era in which businesses are built to operate cleanly, transparently, and defensibly from the moment they are created.

An AI-first compliance model begins with the assumption that regulation will only become more complex, more automated, and more unforgiving. Governments are digitizing faster than businesses, deploying real-time reporting systems, data matching, and predictive enforcement. In this environment, human-centered compliance is structurally incapable of keeping pace. AI-first businesses accept this reality and respond by embedding regulatory logic directly into workflows. Sales systems know tax consequences at checkout. Payroll systems understand reporting thresholds before payments are issued. Accounting systems classify transactions based on compliance impact, not just bookkeeping categories. Nothing happens without regulatory awareness.

This model fundamentally alters how businesses make decisions. Instead of asking, "Is this allowed?" after the fact, leaders see regulatory implications before actions are taken. AI systems simulate outcomes in advance, showing how choices affect filings, exposure, and risk. This transforms compliance into a design constraint that can be optimized, not feared. Businesses choose structures, markets, and growth strategies with full visibility into regulatory consequences, eliminating guesswork and reducing uncertainty at every stage.

AI-first compliance also eliminates the traditional boundary between compliance and strategy. In older models, compliance teams reacted to strategic decisions made elsewhere in the organization. In AI-first businesses, compliance intelligence informs strategy in real time. Expansion plans, pricing changes, hiring decisions, and acquisitions are evaluated not just for profitability, but for regulatory efficiency. This alignment creates organizations that grow intelligently, avoiding costly detours and dead ends caused by overlooked obligations.

Another defining feature of the AI-first model is permanence. Compliance is no longer something that must be "cleaned up" periodically. Records are accurate by default. Filings are correct by design. Audit readiness is continuous. This permanence is critical in a world where historical data is never forgotten and enforcement can look back years instantly. AI-first businesses do not rely on memory, spreadsheets, or individual expertise. They rely on systems that preserve truth automatically.

The AI-first model also redefines accountability. Instead of responsibility being scattered across departments and vendors, accountability is centralized within systems that log every decision, calculation, and submission. This creates clarity for leadership, boards, regulators, and partners. When questions arise, answers are immediate and objective. This level of accountability is impossible to achieve consistently with human-driven processes alone.

Most importantly, AI-first compliance reshapes business confidence. Leaders no longer hesitate due to regulatory uncertainty. They act decisively, supported by systems that adapt faster than rules change. This confidence compounds over time, allowing AI-first businesses to outpace competitors who remain trapped in reactive cycles of compliance panic and recovery.

Chapter 10 concludes the book by making one truth unmistakable: AI-first compliance is not a future trend—it is the new baseline for serious businesses. Those who adopt it will operate with clarity, resilience, and trust. Those who resist it will face increasing friction, cost, and risk. Compliance has evolved from an obligation into an operating philosophy. AI is the engine that makes it permanent.

"Built for the World That Came Next"

The company didn't look extraordinary from the outside. No flashy branding. No viral buzz. Just steady growth and quiet confidence. But inside, everything was different. From the first day, it had been built around one principle: the world would only become more regulated, more automated, and less forgiving—and the business would be ready for that world before it arrived.

When Lena founded the company, she ignored conventional advice. Instead of hiring a compliance team later, she designed the business around AI-driven compliance from the beginning. Every system spoke to each other. Every transaction carried regulatory context. Every decision was evaluated not just for profit, but for long-term defensibility. Friends questioned her priorities. Competitors moved faster in the short term. Lena didn't mind. She was building for durability, not headlines.

As the company grew, the benefits became impossible to ignore. While others scrambled to interpret new rules, Lena's systems adjusted automatically. When reporting requirements expanded, filings were already prepared. When enforcement increased, audits passed without friction. There were no late nights, no emergency meetings, no frantic emails to advisors. Compliance was invisible—not because it was ignored, but because it was embedded everywhere.

Then the world shifted. Governments rolled out real-time reporting. Banks tightened requirements. Platforms demanded proof of compliance before allowing access. Entire industries felt the shock. Businesses paused operations, delayed growth, or shut down entirely under the pressure. Lena's company didn't slow down at all. It had been built for this moment.

While competitors struggled, Lena expanded. She entered new markets confidently, knowing the system would handle regulatory complexity automatically. She hired globally without fear. She partnered with institutions that demanded transparency others couldn't provide. Each move widened the gap between her company and the rest of the market. Years later, when analysts studied why her company dominated while others disappeared, they focused on strategy, timing, and leadership. They missed the deeper truth. The company hadn't just survived regulatory change—it had anticipated it. It hadn't adapted under pressure—it had been designed for pressure from the start.

When Lena eventually stepped back, the company continued running flawlessly. Compliance didn't depend on her. Trust didn't depend on relationships. Everything lived in systems that never forgot, never panicked, and never fell behind. The business wasn't just successful—it was inevitable.

Looking back, Lena understood that the greatest decision she ever made wasn't about product or market. It was about architecture. She had built a company for the world that came next—and when that world arrived, her business was already there.

Final Thoughts

The Compliance Revolution Is Already Here

Artificial intelligence has not simply improved compliance—it has permanently redefined it. What once required armies of accountants, lawyers, spreadsheets, reminders, and last-minute corrections can now be executed continuously, accurately, and invisibly by intelligent systems that never sleep, never forget, and never fall behind. Throughout this book, we have explored how AI transforms compliance from a fragile, reactive obligation into a resilient, proactive foundation for modern business. The conclusion is unavoidable: businesses that adopt AI-driven compliance are not just better protected—they are fundamentally better built.

The traditional compliance mindset was shaped by scarcity: limited information, slow reporting cycles, fragmented systems, and human bottlenecks. That world no longer exists. Governments now operate with real-time data, cross-platform verification, algorithmic enforcement, and historical memory that stretches back indefinitely. In this environment, attempting to manage compliance manually is not just inefficient—it is structurally unsafe. AI is not a luxury or an optimization; it is the minimum viable infrastructure for surviving and scaling in the modern regulatory economy.

What makes AI compliance so powerful is not just automation, but integration. Compliance no longer lives at the edges of the business. It is embedded in transactions, payroll, pricing, expansion, hiring, reporting, and strategy itself. AI connects these elements into a single intelligent system that understands regulatory consequences as they occur. This eliminates blind spots, prevents errors before they happen, and replaces anxiety with certainty. Businesses stop asking whether they are compliant and begin operating as if compliance is guaranteed—because structurally, it is.

Equally important is the shift in leadership psychology that AI enables. Fear has long shaped business decisions: fear of audits, fear of penalties, fear of expansion triggering unknown obligations, fear of due diligence exposing hidden weaknesses. AI removes that fear by replacing uncertainty with clarity. Leaders gain confidence not because they hope everything is correct, but because they can see—at any moment—that it is. This confidence unlocks faster decisions, bolder strategies, and more sustainable growth.

AI-driven compliance also reshapes value. Clean records, continuous audit readiness, and transparent reporting are no longer defensive measures; they are assets. They lower the cost of capital, accelerate deals, improve valuations, and attract partners who demand trust at scale. In an economy where information asymmetry is disappearing, businesses that can prove integrity instantly will always outperform those that rely on explanations after the fact.

Perhaps the most important realization is this: compliance is no longer something businesses "handle." It is something businesses are. The architecture you choose—manual versus automated, fragmented versus unified, reactive versus AI-first—determines not just your risk profile, but your ceiling. Companies built on outdated compliance models will struggle increasingly as regulation accelerates. Companies built on AI compliance will not notice the pressure, because their systems are designed to absorb it.

This book was written to provide more than theory. It is a blueprint for building businesses that are clean by design, scalable by default, and trusted automatically. Whether you are an entrepreneur, executive, investor, or advisor, the message is the same: the future belongs to businesses that treat compliance as infrastructure, not afterthought. AI is the tool that makes that future inevitable.

The compliance revolution is not coming. It is already here. The only question left is whether your business is built for it.

www.ingramcontent.com/pod-product-compliance
Ingram Content Group UK Ltd.
Pitfield, Milton Keynes, MK11 3LW, UK
UKHW020155290926
15471UKWH00005B/886

9 798295 593390